# PSALMS

## Ancient Songs, Modern Messages

Crystal and David Colp

warner press®

Warner Press, Inc.
Warner Press and "Warner Press" logo are trademarks of Warner Press, Inc.

*Psalms: Ancient Songs, Modern Messages*
Written by Crystal and David Colp



Requests for information should be sent to:

Warner Press, Inc
2902 Enterprise Drive
P.O. Box 2499
Anderson, IN 46018
www.warnerpress.org

Editors: Karen Rhodes, Julie Campbell
Cover Designer: Curtis Corzine
Layout: Katie Miller

ISBN: 978-1-68434-174-0
Printed in the USA

Printed in USA

warner press®

# Table of Contents

## A Letter of Introduction

We realize we have only skimmed the surface of the Book of Psalms. There is so much more to be gleaned from this beautifully written book in the Old Testament. Our prayer, however, is for God to do a unique work in your life—just as He did in ours and in the lives of our church family.

God convicted us, healed us, encouraged us, and grew us as we studied these particular chapters in Psalms. We are thankful for the way He spoke and will forever be changed by the specific revelations He provided for us during a difficult time in the life of our church body.

This study came slowly. Every time we thought we could finish it, the enemy threw another obstacle in our path. I believe he wanted it to go unfinished. I believe he worked overtime in our ministry life to keep us busy and distracted so this study would not be completed.

But, God! He provided much needed revelation and time near the end so it could in fact be finished. The difficulty with which this study was finalized leads me to believe there is significant work to be done in the lives of those who will walk the journey through this study with an open, honest, willing heart.

Surrender your preconceived notions of where you are with God, and let Him do something new in you as you study this with us. Revival is on the other side of surrender, and it happens one heart at a time! Let it begin in you!

These ancient songs have a relevant, modern-day message just for you! Are you ready?

Believing revival is on the horizon,

Crystal & David Colp

# Lesson 1: A Community Lament

## Psalm 85

While there is some debate over who actually penned Psalm 85, one could say this is a community lament that spans time and speaks even to the lament of a present day world in turmoil. The Israelites had just returned home from a season of captivity in Babylon to find their homeland in ruins; however, this psalm also speaks to the place we return to after the bondage of sin. Whether you look at this song in the literal or the figurative nature, the message is the same. Restoration is possible in the care of a loving God. As we walk this journey through the psalms, we will place ourselves squarely in the shoes of the people we read about, relating to their circumstances, but also pausing and listening to how the psalms can speak to us today.

**Read Psalm 85 and write down your initial thoughts.**

Psalm 85 was written following a time of exile for God's people. The Israelites had rebelled against the Lord. They had become an adulterous nation, giving themselves to false gods and forsaking their covenant with the Lord. They had completely turned their backs on God. Due to their disobedience, they had been defeated by their enemies, uprooted from their homes, and carried off into slavery. Finally, their exile had ended and some had returned to Jerusalem. But they returned only to see their homes destroyed, their city in shambles, and their temple reduced to a pile of rubble.

As a community, they are deeply traumatized, hurt, and full of sorrow, not knowing which way to turn. They know they have messed up. They recognize their ruined lives are due to their own rebellion, and they want to start over. So, they come together—a community of broken people—seeking the Lord's face again. What we see is not hopelessness, not a spirit of defeat. Instead, we see hope in their hearts—that they might see God move among them like He did in the past, bringing revival and restoration.

**Read Psalm 85:1–3 again and write down the verbs you see in these three verses.**

The people are standing in the ruin of their present circumstances, but they are remembering the past mercies of God. They recall the restoration of the past. They clearly understand they are standing in the midst of rubble, which is the physical manifestation of their disobedience to God. Their present circumstances underscore their sin and rebellion, and yet they know they have a loving, restoring God who has walked beside them time and time again. God is faithfully restoring them, forgiving them, blotting out their sin, withdrawing His wrath, and turning from His anger to grant them favor once again. You can clearly see they hope He will do it again.

Often times we find ourselves standing hopeless in the ruin of our own present circumstances. Sin, rebellion, and disobedience underscore the rubble of our lives and the world around us.

**Are you or someone you love experiencing a circumstance that seems or seemed hopeless? If so, write down your experience here.**

For the Israelites, the rubble of their disobedience and resulting bondage was vast. The temple was destroyed, their city reduced to crushed stone, and their homes in shambles. Sin can also leave our lives strewn with the rubble of its aftermath.

**Describe the "rubble" that has come from sin in your life or the life of someone close to you.**

The temptation to stand in the rubble and look out over the landscape of our lives without hope is enormous. In fact, sometimes the heap of garbage left behind from our sin can seem too big, too vast to overcome, and hopelessness takes over.

Hopelessness is a place of bondage to our present circumstances, and one way to break those chains is to remember the faithfulness of God in the past. The Jewish nation remembered the mercies of God in their past, and we must do the same.

**How did God show His mercy in the past, either to you or someone you know?**

Even though the Jewish people knew God had shown mercy in the past, they had returned home to the ruins of their city and the destruction of the walls surrounding it. The sight of the ruins left them feeling vulnerable, afraid, and lost. If we were honest, we would all say we have experienced the same feelings in some form or fashion at some point in our lives. Vulnerable. A little lost. Stalled in our fear. We could probably add some other feelings in the mix: hurt, betrayed, confused, and the list could go on.

**What are some of the feelings you or someone you love have experienced in the rubble of sin?**

Often, we dwell in that place of pain. But what we see in the psalmist is an honest seeking of God's restoration. We find a submissive, humble heart, searching for God's favor in present circumstances.

**Now read Psalm 85:4–7 again. What does the psalmist ask God for?**

The interesting thing here in verses 4 through 7 is the change in tone. The psalmist makes a subtle switch from remembering the mercies of the past to asking for God's new mercies in the Israelites' present circumstances. He cries for God to restore them, to fix what is broken. He asks questions like, "Will you be angry with us forever?" and "Will you not revive us again?" These questions are laced with grief and desperation—crying out for God to have mercy.

**What are some of the questions you have asked God in the middle of your circumstances?**

Satan would love nothing more than for us dwell in our desperation, to set up camp in our shame, grief, and hurt. He would love for us to believe God is angry with us and will stay angry forever.

**Read John 10:10. What does this scripture say about why Jesus came?**

The Word tells us that God is a life-giving God. He sent Jesus so we could have life. And, not just any life. ABUNDANT LIFE! You can be certain, our God is not a God who gives up on His people. He loves you, and He wants abundant life for you. He will restore and revive you and your heart. Find hope in your present circumstances by claiming the abundant life He offers.

**Read 2 Corinthians 5:17. What does this scripture say about new life in Christ?**

God is the giver of new life, of renewed life, of hope, freedom, restoration, abundance, and so much more. We know this, or at least we should know this, and the children of Israel knew it as well.

**Read Psalm 85:8–9. What does God promise to His people?**

**Read Psalm 85:8 again. What action is taken here by the writer of this psalm?**

In verse 8 there is an intentional posture change. This shift in attitude and heart puts the writer of Psalm 85 in a place to hear from God. The psalmist is listening for God's voice in the chaos—that is where the peace comes from—the stillness, the humility, the admitted need for God.

Verse 9 also says if we fear God, salvation is near. This is not fear in the traditional sense of the word. Instead, this is referring to a healthy reverence of God or the attitude of being awestruck by our God. He is standing with us ready, willing, and able to save us if we will just listen, humble ourselves, put down our own agendas, and let Him do His good work. Peace comes when we recognize who God is and who we are not. I think the Jewish people had a strong understanding of this fact in the first few moments of gazing over the horizon of their lost homes and ruined city. They realized that only God could restore it. Only God could calm their fears and make them whole again.

There is a lesson here for us as well. God is still on the throne, but is He on the throne of our lives? Is He in charge? Can we let go of what we think the restoration process should look like and submit to His perfect plan? The process of humbling ourselves and letting go of our expectations for our lives is not accidental. We, too, must have an intentional posture change—a posture that puts us in a place to hear from Him. Our hearts and attitudes should move to a place of awe, a place of listening to our God.

Often our prayers are full of our own words. What if we silenced our mouths, our minds, our own desires, and opened our hearts to what God has to say? I am convinced that God is speaking even now, and I think He has much to say about how we can find our way through the debris of our own sinful lives to a place of restoration.

**Take a few minutes and sit in silence. Ask the Lord to speak to you in your present circumstances, then be silent and listen. As you listen, simply write down some of the thoughts that come to mind in the space provided.**

**Now look at the end of Psalm 85:9. What will be the result if we listen to and live in awe of God?**

When we change our posture and become humble, attentive seekers of God, He will dwell in our land. The psalmist makes a bold claim here. It's almost a proclamation. He states with boldness: "God, I know if I fear You—if I stand in humble reverence before You, if I lean in and listen, willing to learn from You—then I know You will dwell with me." The word I love most in the verse is the word "dwell." By definition, the word "dwell" means to live in or stay as a permanent resident.

God will dwell. Not pass through. Not breeze by from a distance. He will dwell. He will stay. Again, there is action needed on our part. Just as the psalmist wrote: God's dwelling place is in the hearts of a humble seeker, a heart that is listening and looking for Him.

The enemy would love nothing more than for us to lock our gaze on the hurt, betrayal, and pain of the sin and brokenness in our lives. But God tells us to change our perspective. God says, "Focus on me so that I can dwell with you."

**What is keeping you from focusing on God?**

**Now read Psalm 85:10–13. What we see in this portion of the psalm are the results of God's glory dwelling in the land. Make a list of those results.**

The benefits of submission are innumerable. These last four verses are prophetic words of hope—a modern message of hope for all of us who are standing in the rubble of our own sin or in the rubble of the sin of another. We will see a new faith in God well up within us. We will experience a transformed, humble heart bound to the heart of God. The Lord will give what is good, and we will see an increase of peace, trust, and joy. God will make a way for us through the rubble of this moment. This is His Word. This is a proclamation for personal and communal revival.

The hopelessness of a war-ravaged people was replaced with the hope of a God-fearing community. The fear of looking out over the crumbled remnants of their city was replaced by the freedom that came as revival in the hearts of a people listening intently to their God.

**Where are you today? Are you grasping the hope, forgiveness, and restoration that comes from listening to the heart of God? Or are you shackled to the shame of sin and the rubble it has left behind in your life?**

In the last few moments we have together in Psalm 85, write down and proclaim where you believe God can take you as He restores what hell has stolen from you. Write your own prophecy of hope, your own personal, modern message inspired by this ancient song!

**Want to study more? Look up the history behind the sons of Korah who penned Psalm 85. Write down what you learn about the authors of this particular psalm.**

# Lesson 2: A Repentant Lament

## Psalm 51

If we would take some time to do a little life assessment, most of us could identify habits or choices in our lives that are both good and bad. We could recognize some good habits like exercising, eating a healthy diet, or making sure we always get a good night's sleep. Upon further evaluation, we could probably also identify some not-so-great decisions like drinking twelve cups of coffee in the morning, texting while we drive, or salting everything we eat. These good choices or habits offer life-enhancing benefits. Exercise can help lower our blood pressure, improve our overall health, and help with weight loss. And, of course, the same is true for the negative choices or habits, which have the potential to harm us—habits that put us in danger like texting and driving.

What about our spiritual habits? We can make positive spiritual choices like a daily quiet time or reading through the Bible in a year. But we can also make negative spiritual choices. Unconfessed sin is one of those negative choices that harms us when we do not take the time to evaluate our lives or to recognize the sin that has taken root in our lives. When we fail to have relationships with people who speak truth into our lives and hold us accountable, we walk around with our masks on as if everything is okay. Secretly, sin is eating us up from the inside out. In this chapter, we will take an honest look at sin and may ask some questions that we find hard or are hesitant to answer. But the greatest seasons of growth often come on the heels of dealing with hard things. So, be open to the voice of God, even if it sounds like conviction.

As we look at Psalm 51, we need to remember it is an ancient song with a modern message for us. The primary author of these ancient songs was King David. God said David was a man after His own heart. But this did not mean David was a perfect man. In David we see a man who reminds us once again that we all have a history with sin.

Most of us probably remember one of the very public chapters of David's life. It is recorded for all to see in the title of Psalm 51: *To the choirmaster. A Psalm of David, when Nathan the prophet went to him, after he had gone in to Bathsheba* (ESV). Long story short, David committed adultery with Bathsheba, and she became pregnant. King David tried to cover it up by having her husband, Uriah, killed. David then married her to hide the sin. From the time of the adultery—the subsequent cover-up murder of Bathsheba's husband, Uriah, through the birth of the child—we see in David the attempt to wear a mask, to cover up the sin, to ignore it rather than deal with it, and to continue as if nothing were going on. David was making a choice to cover up a sin, and this bad choice was eating him alive.

In fact, Psalm 32 addresses some of the negative effects in David's life as a result of his unconfessed sin and cover up.

**Read Psalm 32:3–4. Write down in your own words how you think David is feeling.**

Covering up his sin was eating David alive. But at some point after their child was born, God sent a prophet named Nathan to confront David in his sin. Wow! Can you imagine getting this assignment from God? There probably were not many scenarios where confronting King David in his sin was going to go well for Nathan. But he did what God asked him to do anyway. In the end, God used Nathan to challenge David, and he responded with the powerful expression of remorse, repentance, and brokenness we see recorded in Psalm 51. I can't help but think it was this radical, honest brokenness over his sin that was key to God later saying David is a man "after my own heart" (Acts 13:22 NIV®).

> *As we were writing this study, the three campuses of our church came together in a powerful night of prayer, worship, and confession. We had a cross where people could come, write down a sin or confession on a piece of paper, and nail it to the cross. After that service our church ministry staff began praying over those cards. As I was praying and reflecting on this season in the life of our church, God confirmed in my heart that this was one of the really powerful things God was doing in us. I know He was bringing many of us to a place of looking within, evaluating, and if necessary, confessing our own sin. In fact, I had one of the men in our church whose walk with the Lord I really trust, tell me the Lord had laid it on his heart to tell me that God was breaking chains in many lives in our church family.*—**David**

There is power in confession. There is power in repentance. There is power in brokenness before the Lord. This week we are going to let David, chief of sinners, master of the cover up, who ultimately repents and confesses, lead us to this same place of life-changing, chain- breaking confession and repentance.

**Read Psalm 51 and write down your initial thoughts.**

In verses 1 and 2, we see David beginning with what he had come to recognize as his only hope: confession and repentance. David had gone from a common shepherd boy, the youngest in a family of warriors—a boy whose own family couldn't see his leadership potential—to a meteoric rise to fame and power. He was the king! He had developed an impressive resumé: lion and bear killer, fearless warrior, and giant slayer. He had proven himself in the former king's court. He had a distinguished military career prior to becoming king. Over and over again he had seen the enemies of his nation defeated. Then we find him here being confronted with his sin, yet we do not see the arrogant rantings of a prideful king.

**Look at Psalm 51:1–3 again. How would you describe the posture of King David?**

David is not dealing with his sin by minimizing it. He isn't dealing with it by blaming someone else. David isn't putting it on the scale of good deeds compared to bad deeds, saying to God, "Remember all the great things I have done, all the enemies I have defeated, all the inspiring worship songs I've written, all the times I fearlessly followed your lead into battle." He isn't saying, "Look God, surely my good deeds outweigh this one mistake." That was not David's perspective. And that brings up a good point: Perspective is important. When we look at our sin through the lens of serving an almighty God of mercy and love, it should change the way we perceive and react to unconfessed sin in our lives.

**Read Romans 12:2. How do we test and approve what God's will is?**

**Is there anything in your own life right now you feel may be outside of God's best for you?**

A renewed mind is key to discovering what God's best is for our lives. When our minds are set on things of God, we change how we perceive the world around us and the way we interact with it.

**Read Colossians 3:1–10. Describe how we are to live once we have been "made alive" in Christ.**

Going back to David in Psalm 51, we see his humble reaction to his sin, and we also see a perspective that does not minimize what he has done but instead sees sin for what it is. Most often we want to minimize and rationalize away the severity of sin. Our world tells us sin is not a big deal. In fact, the world would prefer that we not even talk about sin. We are made to believe that sin is an outdated concept. Culture would have us reclassify sin or rename it:

"It's not sin; it was a mistake."
"It's not sin; it is simply abnormal social development."
"It's not sin; no one was hurt so that makes it okay."
"It's not pride; it's called having a healthy self-image."
"It's not materialism; it's just living the good life."
"It's not disobedience; I just have a few shortcomings."
"It's not adultery; I am in pursuit of my true soulmate."

**Read Psalm 51:3–5. What does David say about his sin?**

David is acknowledging the depth of his sin. He knows very well that God has every right to pronounce judgement on him. The judgment that he deserved was the sentence God gave at the beginning of time in the garden when Adam and Eve sinned. David understood the total depravity he was born into. Understanding this was important for King David, and it is important for us. Again, perspective matters. We must see our sin for what it truly is in order to experience the freedom that can come on the other side of forgiveness.

**Write down any sin in your life you have been unwilling to acknowledge. Or, maybe there is something you have been unwilling to grasp the depth of, unwilling to acknowledge the damage it is doing to your life. Write down your thoughts here. If you don't feel comfortable writing it down, draw a symbol you will understand, then pause and confess it in prayer. (Remember that accountability is vital for a healthy Christian walk. We would recommend you find someone you can trust to share what God is doing in your life and where you struggle.)**

Freedom and forgiveness first begin with confession. The Holy Spirit convicts, but we also have an action step to take: confession. Confession flows best from a repentant, humble, contrite heart. Writing down or sharing our struggles can be the freeing, first step back to the joy of our salvation!

**Read Psalm 51:7–12. What does David ask God to do?**

Hyssop was a branch from a plant the priest would use in proclaiming someone clean. An animal was sacrificed before the priest, then a hyssop branch was dipped in the blood of the animal and applied to the person as a way of confirming him or her clean. When David writes this in verse 7, in essence he is asking God to pronounce him clean from his sins. As believers under the New Covenant, we understand the visual on an even deeper level when we recognize our need for the blood of another, namely Jesus, to be applied to our lives to cleanse us. David knew he needed to be cleansed from his sins and so do we.

In verse 8, David's tone shifts. He begins to proclaim and pray for what can come from a repentant heart. He begins to see beyond the sin through the lens of God's forgiveness. He is thinking about the forgiveness and grace that God has the power to apply to his repentant life. Joy, gladness, and rejoicing are all things a repentant person could experience, and he longs for all that comes with forgiveness and freedom from sin. He longs to be at peace with himself and God once more.

**Read Psalm 103:12 and Psalm 51:9. What do these two scriptures say about confessed and forgiven sin?**

*Isaiah 43 is one of my favorite chapters in all of the Bible. It begins with a proclamation of redemption and relationship. I love the thought that my God calls me by name because I am His! The chapter goes on to speak of His presence with us as we walk through raging waters and fires blaze around us. He speaks of doing new things, and then just three verses from the end, He makes this statement:* I, even I, am he who blots out your transgressions, for my own sake, and remembers your sins no more*. As if blotting out my sin was not enough, He forgets it, too. Oh, how I wish I could pray for a holy amnesia, to forget my own past, my own sin. But maybe God knows that on some level we need to remember lest we forget just how amazing it is that He forgets.*
**—Crystal**

Psalm 51:10–12 is an intimate moment between David and God, when David takes the step of praying for restoration. Because of his sin, David's heart was grieved as was God's heart. On the other side of repentance and confession, just after praying for joy and gladness, he backtracks and prays for the things that could in fact restore his joy once again. He prays for God to recreate a clean heart and a right spirit within him in verse 10. Then in verse 11 his heart for the presence of God in his life is laid bare for all to see. His desperation to stay connected to his Father is apparent. In essence, David recognizes, he cannot go it alone. This powerful king recognizes his need for the presence of God in his life.

There is so much to learn from David in this psalm, and this is one of the biggest lessons: Pray for a deep, abiding relationship with God. Tell God what you desire in your walk with Him. Tell Him your heart longs for His presence. Ask Him to clean your heart and renew your spirit. Ask Him to give you a desire to spend time with Him. Tell Him how you feel, then ask Him to make it new. Pray for restoration in intricate detail.

**Take a cue from King David. Pause now and pray this prayer or write one of your own:**

God, clean up my heart,
and give me a new, unwavering spirit.
I confess my sins to You, and I ask for Your forgiveness.
Protect me from the guilt of sin weighing me down
and calling me back to a place I left behind.
Thank You for the sacrifice of Your Son, my Savior.
Please be with me. Don't fail to be present,

And do not keep Your Holy Spirit from me.
Restore in me the joy that I once had in Your salvation.
Give me a willing spirit, an open heart to hear Your voice
that will sustain me through even the hardest of days.
I will live a life that will show others Your ways,
so they will turn back to You.
I will speak of how good You are.
Open my lips, Lord.
Give me a boldness to live like You, to be like You.
You don't want just a Sunday morning believer,
You want more. You don't want me to just do things for You.
You want me to spend time with You.
You want my everything. You want my everyday life.
So, Father I will give You a broken spirit;
a broken and humble heart.
I know this is what You want from me,
and this is what I offer.
Grow in me the desires of Your heart.
Amen.

David's prayer of restoration and relationship was not where it ended; we also see a heart willing to share what He had found with others.

**Read Psalm 51:13. What does David say he will do and for what purpose?**

**Read Matthew 28:19–20. What does Jesus ask His disciples to do?**

King David understood clearly that his life was not his own. He knew there was purpose in his salvation, in his restoration. He knew if he could be restored, his life could draw others into relationship with the God he knew and loved. You see, the power of forgiveness reaches beyond the walls of our own hearts. When others see the change in our lives and the joy we find in our relationship with God, it is contagious. The call to be a carrier of God's love is for every believer.

**Read the following scriptures and write what we are to do with our faith.**

**1 Timothy 4:12**

**Matthew 5:16**

**Ephesians 5:1**

Psalm 51 is challenging on several levels. King David teaches us many things in nineteen verses. He is an open book to those who read the words he penned so long ago. Even in his words of confession, he leads us to the God he loves, while understanding the consequences of sin and the freedom in forgiveness, and we must do the same.

We cannot speak of the beauty of who God is without also speaking of the beauty and the sorrow of the sacrifice and why it was necessary. So, while we know this chapter was "heavy," we also know it was needed. Revival follows repentance, forgiveness follows confession, and freedom follows obedience. And from all of this flows the contagious life of a follower of the King of Kings.

**In your last few moments of study and quiet, use the space provided to write a prayer of sorrowful confession and lament, and a declaration of fervent, intentional obedience. Write the prayer, then thank God for His forgiveness and relentless love. Leave it at His feet and take your first step toward personal revival!**

Blessings, sweet friends!

# Lesson 3: A Trust Lament

## Psalm 23

We ended the last lesson in a posture of confession. The hopeful end result was a new place of intentional obedience and a heart of thanksgiving for God's relentless love. Now we step into an expression of trust—a song written to verbally proclaim the comfort the psalmist finds in His God—a popular psalm from generation to generation.

What would you rank as the most popular song of your generation? If you are a "Baby Boomer," it might be "The Twist" by Chubby Checker or "I Want to Hold Your Hand" by the Beatles. For Generation X, it would quite possibly be "Livin' on a Prayer" by Bon Jovi. Millennials might choose "Baby" by Justin Bieber. These songs would more than likely be up for debate, depending on what generation you are from and what your taste in music is. Nevertheless, every generation has its favorites.

The psalms are the songs of God's people. And we could definitely make the case that the greatest hit of the Book of Psalms would be Psalm 23 (at least for the last 1000 years).

**Read Psalm 23 and write down your initial thoughts and impressions.**

Let's look at the first phrase of Psalm 23: *The Lord is my shepherd.* This metaphor of God as our Shepherd is familiar. It is a metaphor we see throughout Scripture, which seems to beg the question, "If God is our Shepherd, then what does that make us?" The answer, of course, is the sheep.

From Genesis, when Jacob declared from his deathbed that God had been his Shepherd throughout his life to Revelation where we read, *For the Lamb in the midst of the throne will be their shepherd* (7:17, ESV)—and a score of places in between—we see the imagery of God as our Shepherd. This recurring message has strong implications in our Christian walk. It is an issue of trust, a relinquishing of our own plans, our control, to the guidance and protection of One greater than us.

As we walk through this psalm together, two questions need to be asked and answered:

1. Is God your Shepherd?
2. Are you following the Shepherd?

Don't answer these questions yet. Just ponder them in your heart as we study Psalm 23 together.

**Psalm 23 was written by someone who knew what it was like to be a shepherd—King David. We meet David for the first time in 1 Samuel 16. Read the following scriptures, and write your impressions of David and how the Bible presents the role of shepherd.**

**1 Samuel 16:1–13**

**1 Samuel 17:34–35**

David understood the role of a shepherd. He knew part of his job was to protect and care for the sheep, so when he described God as his Shepherd he understood distinctly what it meant. At the point of penning this psalm, God had proven Himself over and over again to David as his good and faithful Shepherd.

**Read 2 Samuel 22:1–20 and write down how God was a Shepherd for David.**

Commentators actually believe this psalm was written later in David's life, possibly during the rebellion of his son Absalom, when he tried to steal David's throne.

**Read 2 Samuel 15:1–13. Write down how Absalom gained followers.**

Absalom started a great rebellion, causing David to fear for his life. In the end, Absalom was killed, and David retained the throne. David's heart was grieved. He had hoped to avoid Absalom's death because he loved him, though Absalom had proven to be wicked. So much life experience flowed from David's pen as he wrote the words to Psalm 23.

> *I think David's words,* "The Lord is my shepherd," *are rooted in several emotions. Excitement and pride that the all-powerful, all-knowing, Creator God, the only true God was willing to care for David as his Shepherd. He was grateful that the holy, righteous God of the universe didn't give up on him, but left the 99 in pursuit of David, bringing him back into the fold. David did not see His God as an impersonal, aloof, blind watchmaker who wound up the universe and was off to other more important matters. "No," David says, "The Lord is MY Shepherd."*
> **—David Colp**

What about you? How do you feel about the Good Shepherd? You may be walking a difficult road you feel God or the Bible cannot really speak to. I would challenge you to read Psalm 23 within the context that it was written. David knew what it was to have a rebellious child; although, I doubt any of us can comprehend a child so rebellious they try to dethrone us and kill us in the process. Yet God proved trustworthy. David knew what it was to wander away from God and commit adultery, only to have the Good Shepherd continue to pursue him and care for him. King David knew what it was to be comforted and protected by his Shepherd when the wolves and lions were all around him. David had been led by the Good Shepherd, made to lie down by the Shepherd, led by the still waters, in paths of righteousness, his soul restored by his Shepherd. You can know this Shepherd's care, too!

The old adage of "been there, done that, got the T-shirt" is an understatement concerning David and his on again-off again relationship with God. There is nothing you are going through that God cannot be trusted with. You can never run so far from God that He won't pursue you.

Trust, or rather the lack of it, is often at the core of our running from God. This happens to everyone. We all struggle sometimes with a lack of trust. Nobody is perfect. But, the road back does take work. The beginning point is confession, which you just did in the last lesson. One of the next steps is remembering what He has already done for you. In Psalm 23, King David is doing exactly that—remembering and declaring who his Good Shepherd is and what He has done and will do in his life. Let's follow David's lead and do the same.

**In what ways has God been your Good Shepherd?**

**In what areas of your life do you need to trust God and give Him control?**

Sometimes we don't realize that we forfeit a tremendous amount of peace when we refuse to lean in and let God shepherd us. With trust there also comes the relief of letting go. In the trust zone it's okay to "lie down in green pastures."

One of the key jobs of a shepherd is to find good pastures for his sheep. Sheep only lie down when they are content. If they are anxious in any way—whether hungry or afraid of nearby predators—they will not lie down. They lie down only when they are at ease and when they feel safe. The Good Shepherd provides an environment for them to lie down—when the shepherd is near they are safe.

You see, the proximity of the shepherd matters. When he is near, the sheep know they can lie down in safety. Think about our own lives. Life throws a lot at us. We experience any number of dangers: financial danger, dangers to our health, relationships, hopelessness, etc. But when we are dwelling in close proximity to our God, even when life is not perfect, we can be content knowing He is with us.

**Read Psalm 4:8 and write down your thoughts.**

*I had the flu recently, and let me tell you, it was the worst case of the flu since the nightmarish Thanksgiving flu outbreak at the Colp house in 2000. It was a Wednesday morning, and I woke up not feeling well. I was a bit sick to my stomach first thing, but I decided to go to the gym anyway. Once I got to the gym, I ended up in the bathroom, but I chalked it up to the fact of working out so hard at 6:30 a.m. The cell phone was ringing,*

*but I was not picking up. I did as much of the workout as I could. I drove home, feeling worse and worse. Once I pulled into the driveway, I opened my door and immediately got sick. I felt better after that, so I once again made an excuse for the whole episode and proceeded to eat breakfast. (Bad idea #47 of the day!) Crystal left for the office as she had meetings all day long. I now felt absolutely horrible. I could not walk more than a few steps without getting sick. Wave after wave of nausea set in, and as I lay on the bathroom floor, I just wanted Crystal to be home. Even though I knew there was nothing she could do, I just wanted her to be close.*
**—David**

Sometimes just knowing the shepherd is near makes life's toughest moments better. As my Good Shepherd, God creates an environment where I can lie down and trust He is in control. I can "lie down in green pastures." His presence makes all the difference.

**Are you dwelling in close proximity to the Good Shepherd? If so, how do you remain near Him? If not, what is keeping you far from Him?**

St. Augustine said, "Thou hast made us for thyself, O Lord, and our heart is restless until it finds its rest in thee." Finding the place of rest in the Good Shepherd isn't always easy. Our restless souls cause us to wander, but what if we were to pray the words from the old hymn *Come Thou Fount of Every Blessing*?

"Lord, bind my wandering heart to thee."

The good news: He is in the business of restoring souls. Even though we may be following the Good Shepherd closely, there will be times when we need to be restored. Life has a way of sneaking up on us.

**Read Psalm 42:11. Write down a time in your life when you felt just like the psalmist feels in this verse.**

In this verse, the psalmist points to the restoration the Good Shepherd provides. All of us, no matter how spiritually fat and sassy we are, can walk through seasons where we become spiritually anemic, where we lose our way. We are prone to wander. Scripture says, *All we like sheep have gone astray* (Isaiah 53:6, ESV). There are times when we need to be reminded of the close proximity of our Good Shepherd, because we forget.

**Read the following scriptures and write down what they have to say about the nearness of God:**

**Psalm 34:18**

**Psalm 145:18**

**Jeremiah 23:23**

**James 4:8**

**Romans 8:35, 37–39**

Isn't it good to be reminded that He is near? He is near and ready to lead us like the Good Shepherd He is, in paths of righteousness–for His name's sake.

> *I love to talk about my God...to read about Him. I love the reminders of His goodness, His provision, His leading, His help, His strength—I love all of that. But, sometimes I think we get overly caught up in all He does for us, forgetting about the fact that it's not just for us. Oh, don't get me wrong. God is a good Father, and just like any daddy He enjoys giving good things to His children. But at the end of the day, it's all about Him. It's about His name. The good He does for us is an opportunity to bring glory to His name so others can see Him in tangible ways. We do have a responsibility to share what He has done for His name's sake. To see His name glorified, lifted up to draw all men to Him! Living a life of joy and thanksgiving, a life readily acknowledging He is our Good Shepherd is a contagious life. For His Name's Sake...that's the life I want to live.*
> **—Crystal**

Often, our lives speak of anything *but* the Good Shepherd, so as I read Psalm 23 it is the declaration of a man desiring nothing more than to follow the shepherd. Even though we know King David failed miserably at times to follow the leading of his God, he never stopped declaring and speaking about the type of sheep he wanted to be. He was an imperfect person who kept coming back, a man the Good Shepherd kept going after.

All of this simply means the Good Shepherd, God, wants a relationship with you—a deep, abiding relationship—one of trust and surrender, where He leads, guides, protects, and provides. The result is goodness and mercy following us all the days of our lives, and in the end we will dwell in the house of the Lord forever!

**In the beginning we asked two questions. Now it's time to answer:**

**Is God your Shepherd?**

**Are you following the Shepherd?**

2 Samuel 22:1–20 (GNT) says, *The Lord is my protector; he is my strong fortress. My God is my protection, and with him I am safe. He protects me like a shield; he defends me and keeps me safe. He is my savior; he protects me and saves me from violence. I call to the Lord, and he saves me from my enemies. Praise the Lord! The waves of death were all around me; the waves of destruction rolled over me. The danger of death was around me, and the grave set its trap for me. In my trouble I called to the Lord; I called to my God for help. In his temple he heard my voice; he listened to my cry for help. Then the earth trembled and shook; the foundations of the sky rocked and quivered because God was angry! Smoke poured out of his nostrils, a consuming flame and burning coals from his mouth.*

*He tore the sky open and came down, with a dark cloud under his feet. He flew swiftly on his winged creature; he traveled on the wings of the wind. He covered himself with darkness; thick clouds, full of water, surrounded him; burning coals flamed up from the lightning before him. Then the LORD thundered from the sky, and the voice of Almighty God was heard. He shot his arrows and scattered his enemies; with flashes of lightning he sent them running. The floor of the ocean was laid bare, and the foundations of the earth were uncovered when the LORD rebuked his enemies and roared at them in anger. The LORD reached down from above and took hold of me; he pulled me out of the deep waters. He rescued me from my powerful enemies and from all those who hate me—they were too strong for me. When I was in trouble, they attacked me, but the LORD protected me. He helped me out of danger; he saved me because he was pleased with me.*

**This was a song David wrote in response to his Good Shepherd when God spared him. At the end of this lesson in Psalm 23, it would be fitting to write your own psalm, declaring God as your Good Shepherd. Use the space below to write a prayer, a song, a poem, or your thoughts of God as your Good Shepherd! Compose your very own lament of trust!**

Any time you doubt or fear, come back to this. Remember, this is a message that defies time, an ancient song with a modern message: God is worthy of our trust, He is the Good Shepherd we all need, and you can never wander too far for Him to find you!

# Lesson 4: A Didactic Psalm

## Psalm 78

God is a gentle guiding shepherd. He leads and teaches along the way. One example of a way He uses His Word to teach us is through specific portions of scripture. A didactic psalm is one written for the purpose of teaching, or to impart wisdom from the teacher or writer to the student or reader of the written word. It may tell stories or parables to make a point. In Psalm 78 the writer shares the story of a rebellious people and their propensity toward sin. In essence, he is sharing the sinful journey of a group of people in an effort to prevent the next generation from making the same mistakes.

**Read Psalm 78 in its entirety. Write down your thoughts as you read.**

The culture we live in today thrives on information. The Internet has made information readily accessible and vast. Social media is a big part of this age of information we live in. We parade the best parts of our lives, giving everyone the perception that our life is perfect and void of fault. We enjoy wearing masks, only allowing people access to what we want them to see. When struggle enters our lives, we shove it down and hide it, claiming we are strong enough to handle it on our own. This is faulty reasoning on many fronts.

**Why do you think it's healthier for us to be honest about where we are and what we are struggling with?**

**Read Leviticus 26:39–42. What is the result when all generations repent of their sins?**

The effects of sin can linger from generation to generation, even when one generation does its best to prevent the next from making the same mistakes. We are really good at not listening, doing our own thing, and making our own mistakes. But sharing honestly with others about our own imperfections and struggles can be valuable. This honesty opens doors for people to find help when they truly understand they do not walk alone. When they see God's grace and forgiveness at work in your life, they find hope for their own circumstances.

Is there someone in your life or sphere of influence who might benefit from hearing your grace story or your own personal didactic psalm? If so, who?

**Write the name or initials of that person and a prayer that God would open a door for you to share, in love, what God has brought you through to help him or her find the way home.**

Sharing our pain and recovery from past sin is important and can be helpful, but let me warn you—there can be a right time and a wrong time to share. It is vitally important to stay deeply connected with the Father, praying for wisdom to know when it is right and restraint for the moments when it is wrong. There is an old saying, "You must earn the right to be heard." Earning this right takes time and a love investment in the life of the person you feel might benefit from your journey.

Trust me when I say this is not an overnight trip. Sometimes it takes years to get to a place where you can share, but it is so worth the effort to see a soul won for the Lord.

Redeeming your story is the true nature of a testimony. The enemy hates this because he would rather you hide and cower from your past. God says, "I can redeem what the enemy meant for evil." Trust God and share your story!

**Write your redemption story here. Some advice: When sharing your story, keep it under five minutes, don't get lost in the details, and finish with examples of God's love, forgiveness, and power in your life. It would also be prudent for you to share this with someone you trust to give you honest feedback before sharing it with someone you hope to win to the Lord.**

**Read the following scriptures and write down what we should tell the next generation.**

**Psalm 78:4–6**

**1 Peter 2:9**

**Psalm 145:3–4**

**Psalm 71:18**

**Deuteronomy 6:5–7**

In Psalms, there are many examples of the writer proclaiming the goodness of God. We see this example throughout scripture, even outside the Book of Psalms. You see, telling your story of redemption is important, but it is also important to simply share the greatness of our God.

> *I think as humans our default setting is negative, especially when life goes awry, not quite the way we think it should go. I have found that when I look for God in a situation I can find Him. But I have to be willing*

*to look. Sometimes it's a scavenger hunt and other times He has been at work right in front of me, but I couldn't see through the fog of sin, anxiety, stress, pain, illness, or just a plain old bad attitude. When I do find Him at work, even in the smallest of situations, my perspective changes. My mind can then see the positive and find peace even when life is hard. The way I see it, we either proclaim His goodness, power, and mercy with our lives, or we deny it. I don't know about you, but I would so much rather be a billboard for the greatness of my God than a straw, sucking the life-giving marrow of my Holy God from the lives of others by how I live.* **—Crystal**

This becomes a teaching moment as well, a moment when our didactic life psalm shares the wisdom of worship with those around us. If we claim to be children of God, our lives speak of Him whether we realize it or not. We trumpet His greatness or we live out our own hypocrisy, casting a long shadow over the God we claim to serve. These are sobering thoughts, but necessary for us to process as a part of our growth as followers of Jesus.

**Read Psalm 78 once again. This time write down what God did for His people.**

The writer of this psalm does something unique. He tells a story to teach. He weaves the disobedience of God's people with the compassion of a loving, great God and mixes in a dash or two of the judgment of a righteous God. As you read this story, if you are paying attention, you learn a great deal—not only about disobedience but also about God Himself.

The author of this psalm is thought to be Asaph. Asaph was a Levite who was in the service of King David. He served as a music leader and a teacher. He belonged to the tribe of Levi, and one of their jobs was to teach.

As Asaph communicates, he leaves you with the sense that there are gems of truth wrapped in a history lesson of sorts. If you read Psalm 78 slowly and with the eyes of your heart open, you see this is a historically accurate account of the relationship between God and the nation of Israel. He is using history to teach a greater spiritual lesson to the next generation. Asaph sees the history and lessons found there to be important to the student.

In 1905, author George Santayana said, "Those who cannot remember the past are condemned to repeat it." Asaph was well aware of this. He knew the nation well and understood their track record of forgetting the God they served. The urgency in his voice is almost palpable. He is desperate for the generation following him to learn from the mistakes of the past so history would not repeat itself.

This is the way history should be taught. Sometimes the past is ugly. Sometimes it is saturated with greed, ignorance, cruelty, hatred, division, sin—the list could go on and on, but it is important for every generation to understand and avoid the faults of the previous one. If we scrub biblical, familial, or world history in an effort to make it palatable and less offensive, we are robbing it of the teachable moments, thus putting us in danger of repeating it. You can communicate history, robbing it of truth, or you can communicate history, teaching its truth in a way that challenges the next generation to a higher level. This was the heart of Asaph, and this must be the heart of the church.

We cannot rob the gospel of the truth of the blood of Jesus or the truth of sin and the consequences of it. These truths must both challenge the next generation to a higher standard of holiness and embrace the fine line we walk between grace and truth. Asaph struck this chord well, and we must find a way for the next generation to do the same.

Let's spend some time talking about how we handle the truth and the opportunities God provides for us to share it with others.

**Read the following scriptures, and write down how these words should affect the way we communicate the truth of the gospel.**

**2 Timothy 2:15**

John 1:14

John 8:31–32

1 Corinthians 13:4–6

2 Peter 1:20–21

Hebrews 4:12

Often times we choose to share what we deem as "truth" in the heat of a difficult moment. Unfortunately, we believe dropping a "truth bomb" on a difficult person is necessary to open their eyes to their depravity. Instead, what we cause is clenched eyes—shut to the truth out of hurt and an inability to hear the concern in our voices—because our lack of grace is louder.

Let me interject here: We are all teachers in one form or another. If we truly want to train the next generation, we must get a thorough handle on what we are trying to teach them. We cannot teach them out of ignorance, but rather out of a heart filled with grace and a mind steeped in God's truth. We must teach from a place of relationship—relationship with God, relationship with others, and a relationship with His Word.

In teaching the next generation, the life you live out loud is most important. Second in importance is what you communicate to them verbally. They will not hear you if they don't see you living out what you are saying. Asaph lived life in the service of not only King David but also God. He served in the temple, following strict guidelines and historically giving up rights to own land. His life exemplified what he taught.

**Read the following verses, and write down what they say about how we should live out our lives as believers.**

**Psalm 16:11**

**1 Peter 1:15–16**

**Psalm 119:9**

**Philippians 2:5**

**Romans 12:1**

This is not meant to discourage but instead to encourage you toward a life that looks more and more like Jesus every day. No one is perfect except for Jesus Christ, but God does ask us to allow Him to challenge and change us as we grow up in Him. Your journey will look different than mine. The Holy Spirit will walk with you and talk with you about your relationship with God, convicting you when there is something you need to work on. The key is to be humble and vulnerable enough to allow Him access to every nook and cranny of your life so you can work together. I guess this is a challenge for all of us to take stock of what we might need to say goodbye to in order to say hello to the best God has for us.

If we listen to Asaph as he taught history in order to teach spiritual lessons to the next generation, we will learn what we need to do in order to avoid the mistakes of the past.

This lesson is simply about three things:

1. Learning from the past
2. Teaching the next generation about the past
3. Living differently than the past

**The way we teach is important and so is the way we live. So, what is God saying to you right now? Write down your thoughts.**

**Now write a prayer asking God to teach you daily as you journey together. Ask Him to open doors for you to share your unique history lesson—your own personal didactic life psalm—with the next generation.**

# Lesson 5: A Psalm of Thanksgiving

## Psalm 46

At the end of Lesson 4, you were challenged to think through your story and ask God to open doors for you to share it with the next generation. Sharing stories of how God has walked with you through life—providing, helping, protecting, and working on your behalf—is a powerful way to communicate His goodness with others. Your God story can be a natural outflow of who you are when you have a humble, thankful heart for all He has done. Psalm 46 is defined as a psalm of thanksgiving.

This psalm and a few others are attributed to "the sons of Korah." The sons of Korah were from a family known for being jealous of the position Moses had among God's people. In a nutshell, Korah and some others took a stand against Moses, but his sons did not. The sons of Korah made the right decision to honor God above the need for high position and notoriety. Korah and his supporters angered God, the earth opened and swallowed Korah and all his compatriots, but his sons were spared. When you see statements such as, *Therefore we will not fear, though the earth gives way* (Psalm 46:2, NIV), understand these men knew what it was to see the earth give way. Yet, they still proclaimed their God is a refuge and a help in times of trouble. Few of us can claim the trouble their family line had endured, seeing their fathers swallowed by the earth, but they declared with a thankful heart the power and goodness of God in this psalm.

**For deeper study, do some research on the sons of Korah and write down your findings here.**

**Read Psalm 46 in its entirety. Write down your thoughts as you read.**

**Write Psalm 46:1 in the space provided and underline how God is described.**

*God is our refuge* is a phrase used 94 times in the Old Testament, with 44 of those occurrences in the Book of Psalms. The word *refuge* means someone or something we turn to for assistance, security, and protection from danger or distress. God as our refuge means He will protect us, provide shelter, and fend off our enemies.

The second half of this "God is" statement describes Him as our *strength, an ever-present help in trouble* (Psalm 46:1, NIV®). God's power actively works on our behalf in more of an offensive posture. In short, as we read this psalm, we are reminded of God's help in our struggles.

**Read the following scriptures and write down what they say about our helper God.**

**Isaiah 41:13**

**Isaiah 50:7**

**Nehemiah 8:10**

**John 14:26**

**Hebrews 13:6**

I love the last part of Psalm 46:1. The thought of God being *ever-present* is comforting.

> *When you've faced difficult times, how often have you had someone tell you they would be willing to help, but when help is needed you know they wouldn't actually come through, or even be capable of coming through? God is a present Helper. He is the Friend who is always found—the One*

*who always picks up the phone, responds to your texts, and is always there. We all have different types of friends. We have the moving friends we would reach out to if we were moving. The strong friends, the friends with trucks. We have the "best man" kind of friend, who on our wedding day holds onto the wedding rings and doesn't lose the marriage license. These are the friends you would trust with your life. We have the fishing boat friends, the handyman friends, go-on-vacation-together friends, and on the list could go. We have these people in our lives who are just simply better in some circumstances than others. But God. He is "the-always-there-regardless-of-the-situation friend." He is an always-present, never-fail help.* **—David**

**Write Psalm 46:2 in the space provided and underline what this protection, strength, and help means in your life.**

Verse 2 begins with the word *therefore*. Because God is a refuge, because He is our strength and ever-present help, we do not have to fear.

**Read Psalm 46:2–3 again.**

The continuation of verse 2 into verse 3 gives examples of things we do not have to fear. The psalmist speaks of things like the earth giving way and mountains quaking. Remember the history of the sons of Korah and the trauma they had witnessed in their lives? These events were very real crisis moments for them. And while our crisis moments look different, we all have moments in our lives when we feel like the earth is shifting underneath us and life is shaking to the point of almost breaking apart, causing us to fear.

**Write down some thoughts on what in your life is causing fear now or what has caused fear in the past.**

**Let's put a pin in the causes of our fear for a moment and read Psalm 46:4–7 again.**

In these verses, it seems the psalmist has switched gears and changed subjects mid-stream. This is why digging into God's Word and being able to contextualize the scripture is important. There is deeper meaning here. The psalmist is painting a picture of a God who provides, a God who can make a dry and barren city glad. And the encouragement for us is this: If our God can bring joy to a city, if His voice can melt the earth, then we must believe He will help us.

The city the psalmist refers to here is Jerusalem. In this time period, it is the city where the temple resides, and the Holy of Holies housing the ark of the covenant is within its walls. In essence, the psalmist is saying, "God is within the city and even though this city sits in a dry, barren landscape with very little water, God is a source of living water. And, because the presence of God rests in the temple within the Holy of Holies, He helps her and sustains her."

When a city has a sustainable source of clean water, it has life. The psalmist sings of life, refuge, strength, and help in the presence of his God. You are reading the words of a person who has seen the goodness of God in the past, and now he is writing a song to encourage the people of God to see the same.

**Read John 7:37–38 and write down what Jesus has to say about living water.**

If we believe in Jesus, living water is flowing from our hearts. Relating this thought back to Psalm 46:4–5, we can know there is a river flowing within us as God's children, and the result should be a glad heart. You are the place where the Holy Spirit dwells. God is within you, you will not fail, and He will help you at the break of day. The power of His voice has not changed. When you are a willing vessel of His power, God can and will speak through you, in your circumstances and the circumstances of others. His voice still melts mountains.

**Returning to the pin we put in the fears we listed earlier, what mountain of fear do you need God's voice to melt? What dead, barren wastelands of fear do you need the river of life to sweep over?**

Pause for just a few moments and declare the power of God over this area of fear. Fill in the first blank below with your name, and state your fears in the second blank; then, pray this prayer based on Psalm 46:7 out loud.

> The Lord Almighty is with me, the God of ______________ is my fortress…
>
> Therefore, I will not fear__________________________________ any longer.
>
> God is my refuge and strength.

Praying verse 7 is significant in at least three ways:

1. The word *with* is important, implying the presence of God once again as ever-present.
2. *The God of Jacob* signifies the personal nature of our God and His desire to have a personal relationship with His children.
3. The word used for fortress/refuge in this verse is different than the word used in verse 1. This word means "an inaccessible high place," implying an even greater place of protection.

As you prayed this prayer, you acknowledged His presence with you always. You acknowledged your personal relationship with Him, and you claimed His promise of impenetrable protection against your greatest fears.

Now comes the praise part. This is where thanksgiving enters the picture. Because God is all of this and so much more, He is worthy of praise! The psalmist is reminding God's people to look around, open their eyes, and come and see His greatness.

**Read Psalm 46:8–9. Write down what God has done for His people according to the psalmist.**

The first part of this psalm is a declaration of God as a refuge. The second part is a picture of the glory of God. You can see the writer pointing to the greatness of God and His might, even in the examples he uses of what God has done for them. The Hebrew idea of thanksgiving has to do with who God is, not necessarily what He has done. In verses 8 and 9, the writer does state what God has done, but the examples are strongly tied to His power and His protection. It all relates! Do you see it?

We get so caught up in what God does or doesn't do for us. Our lack of thanksgiving or the plentiful nature of our praise is often conditional upon our view of His provision. What we learn here is that thanksgiving should be determined only by who He is. Because God does not change, neither should our heart of thanksgiving. The bonus here is when we take our eyes off of circumstances and place them squarely on Him alone, we experience a change in perspective. When we have a healthy view of who God really is, our fear doesn't stand a chance in the shadow of the Almighty.

In the last verses of our study on Psalm 46, we read what God says about all of this.

**Read Psalm 46:10 and write it here. Underline what God says we should do.**

Often, when we read the words, *Be still and know that I am God,* we assume this means to take a quiet, contemplative lifestyle. While resting and focusing on God is good, I do not think this is necessarily the emphasis here.

**Read Psalm 46:8–10 in The Message.**

Verse 10 begins: *Step out of the traffic! Take a long, loving look at me, your High God.* When you step out of traffic, it does not cease. The traffic will still be buzzing around, but when you are not standing in the midst of it you're not worried about being hit. When you are not standing in the midst of traffic, your focus can change from carefully watching cars to make sure you are safe, to focusing on other things.

God wants us to realize that all the things we focus on mean nothing in light of who He is. When we step away from what the world is throwing at us right now and look fully at Him, we can see the greatness of our God in comparison to our problems!

Be still and see Him for who He is. Be still and look long enough at Him for your perspective to change. He is above the nations. He is above anything here on earth. He is greater! The big idea is actually surrender—surrendering our own ideas of provision, acknowledging God for who He is, finding confidence in Him—our response is thanksgiving!

> *When I began writing this chapter, I had my own ideas of where this would go. As I dug in and began studying, I realized there was so much more here than our normal idea of what thanksgiving looks like and where it comes from. Most often our moments of thanksgiving are derived out of the good He does for us. Oh, we may speak of His greatness in these moments as well, but they are still deeply rooted in provision or what we perceive as provision. While I think it is important to have a grate-*

*ful heart for what He does, an even deeper thanksgiving comes from a simple place of awe and wonder, or even a place of despair where we must trust Him when the earth is shaking beneath us. To see Him high and lifted up above anything we can see with our earthbound eyes is where the psalmist was aspiring to take us in Psalm 46. He wants us to see our fears in relation to the big God we serve. He wants us to experience a perspective change. When I truly see God for who He is, it drives me to thanksgiving and causes my fears to disappear beneath the glory of my God.* **—Crystal**

**Read the following scriptures and write down what they say about the greatness of God.**

**Isaiah 55:8–9**

**Jeremiah 10:6**

**Psalm 145:3**

**Psalm 147:4–5**

**1 Chronicles 29:11**

This psalm ends with another declaration of God's presence with His people.

**Read Psalm 46:11 and write it here.**

"The Lord of Hosts" refers to the title *Yahweh Sabaoth,* and the idea behind this title is that God is the Commander of armies both in the earthly and heavenly realms. This once again points us to the power, might, and greatness of our God. He is with us, we are in relationship with Him, and He is our protector. This verse, as in verse 7, is a statement of praise and declaration of His greatness, reminding the reader to see God for who He is.

We all need reminders at times, and Psalm 46 is a holy Post-it™ note to stick on the mirror of our hearts prompting us toward surrender, trust, awe, and thanksgiving!

As we end today, let's practice surrender, trust, awe, and thanksgiving. Under each heading, write a prayer. Turn your fears over to Him. Be specific about where you see Him already at work. Declare His greatness. Give Him thanks for who He is to you in spite of your circumstances.

**We surrender our fears:**

**We trust Him to help:**

**We stand in awe of God's greatness:**

**We give thanks for who He is:**

This week, reread the scriptures you looked up on the greatness of God. Choose one of them to memorize, or find one of your own. Try to commit at least one verse to memory that speaks to the greatness of God so you are armed with God's Word when fear tries to rear its ugly head. You can combat it with a dose of scripture, declaring the greatness of God and giving Him thanks for the power at your disposal! Fear is a liar—combat it with a thankful heart, full of the truth of God's Word!

For further inspiration surrounding the idea of thanksgiving being born of awe, listen to the song *Psalm 46 (Lord of Hosts)* by Shane & Shane, released in 2015.

# Lesson 6: A Prophetic Psalm

## Psalm 22

In Lesson 5 we explored thanksgiving with the challenge of a perspective shift in regards to our view of God and putting our fears under the power of our great God. Lesson 6 will ask us to change our gaze once more, this time toward the cross.

We also focused in Lesson 5 on thanking God simply for who He is; now we look toward what He has done for us. Only a great God would weave the story of redemption we have in His Son, Jesus Christ. In His greatness God saw fit to save us.

**Read Psalm 22 in its entirety. Write down your thoughts as you read.**

*Since I was a kid I have loved video games. I got my first gaming system, the original Atari 2600 game console, when I was about 12. Developers started hiding their signatures with an Atari 2600 game called Adventure. Why? Atari leadership wouldn't give the game developers credit for their work back then because they were afraid of the royalties they would have to pay them. If you got to a particular, very difficult place in the Adventure game you would see the message "Created by Warren Robinet." That hidden message became what is now called an "Easter Egg." It was named after the Easter tradition of hunting for and finding Easter eggs. A simple definition of an "Easter Egg" as it relates to video gaming is "a hidden message or feature in a video game." You can find "Easter Eggs" in comics, cartoons, and movies, but you have to be paying attention. In Psalm 22 we see an "Easter Egg," or a hidden message from God to us about Jesus, our Messiah.* **—David**

This psalm, which is considered one of the Messianic psalms, has some important things to teach us about Jesus, specifically Jesus' crucifixion and what His sacrifice on the cross means for us. Psalm 22 is quoted seven times in the New Testament, and each time in reference to Jesus Christ. Look at Psalm 22 and notice the author. This is a psalm of David.

As you read Psalm 22, you will notice it reads like David is writing it while standing at the foot of the cross during Jesus' crucifixion. That wouldn't be a huge deal, except for the fact that David lived roughly 1,000 years before Christ, and he wrote this psalm some 400 or 500 years before the first use of crucifixion as a means of execution. David would have known nothing about crucifixion. Again, let me remind you that this is an *Easter Egg*—a message hidden in the Old Testament pointing us to Jesus, teaching us something about Jesus. We see in Psalm 22 the fingerprints of God and His redemptive work. This psalm points to the miraculous, God-orchestrated sacrifice of Jesus for humanity. This is the *Easter Egg* of all *Easter Eggs*!

Psalm 22 was written by David in the midst of a difficult place in his life. He is feeling everything he expresses in this psalm. We see in Psalm 22 not only the foreshadowing of Jesus but also the immediate relevance to David, who penned this psalm. We will focus on Jesus in this lesson, leaning into the lessons we can learn from Psalm 22 about our Messiah.

**Read the following scriptures and make a note of any similarities between the two.**

### Psalm 22:1–2

### Mark 15:34

Jesus quotes Psalm 22 as He hangs there for several hours, nailed to the cross. Here is Jesus–in relationship with God the Father since before the foundations of this world were laid—on the cross.

**Read John 1:1.**

Jesus is the Word, and before there was anything else, Jesus was with God. Jesus, the Holy Spirit, and God the Father have been together since before time or matter. The Trinity has always been in perfect relationship. Now, as Jesus takes our sin upon Himself, He is separated from God.

**Read Isaiah 59:2. How does sin affect our relationship with God?**

At the moment Jesus takes our sin, He is separated from God. He cries out in anguish. This separation brings deeper anguish, more profound and painful than the beatings and physical suffering He endured. He cries, *My God, My God, why have you forsaken me?* (Mark 15:34, NIV®). This cry comes as He experiences ultimate isolation on the cross.

We have felt separation from God, too. Now, our separation from God in no way rivals the separation the Son of God felt from His Father, but we have nonetheless all felt separated from God at one point or another. There have been situations that pushed us away. Many of the great men and women of faith have recorded seasons where they felt far from God either because of their sin or maybe there was some doubt or struggle in their faith.

We often feel as if no one understands this pain of separation. Then there is Jesus on the cross, crying out in anguish over the separation He feels from His Father. Know today, Jesus understands us. He understands what it feels like not only to have been far from God but also to feel far from His Father.

Knowing that we have a Savior who understands can be a tremendous comfort. It's yet another reminder that Jesus did come to be with us, to live among us, to be tempted like us, to feel all the pain, anguish, and suffering of this world. He even understands what it is like to feel far from God because of sin. It was our sin He took upon Himself, causing the separation from His Father.

**Read 1 Peter 2:22–25. Why did Jesus take on our sins and die on the cross?**

**Now read Psalm 22:5–6. How do you think this refers to Jesus on the cross?**

In this passage, Jesus is being defined as a worm. You can't get much lower and more insignificant than a worm. Scorned and despised is the description, but there is more to see.

There is another word in Hebrew for *worm*. It is a generic word for *worm* more commonly used, but the psalmist, under the inspiration of the Spirit, did not use this Hebrew word. Instead, another word for worm translated in other scripture as *crimson* or *scarlet* was used. This is a word with a dual meaning.

There are a number of places in Exodus where this word is used. It is used when talking about the colors on the tabernacle, and the word is translated *scarlet* in Exodus 35.

In ancient times a red or scarlet worm would be crushed in order to dye things red. When the female worm of this species was about to give birth, which she does one time in her life, she attaches to a piece of wood. She then builds a hard crimson shell and lays her eggs under the protective shell. The eggs eventually hatch, and for three days they feed on the mother worm. As she dies she oozes scarlet on them and on the wood.

With the mother worm now dead, the shell turns a waxy white color and flakes off on the ground. She gives her life so they can live.

**Read Isaiah 1:18. Write down the similarities between the story of the crimson worm and what this scripture says.**

**Write down the similarities you see in the story of the crimson worm and what Jesus did for us.**

Jesus intentionally gave His life. He willingly attached himself to a piece of wood, just like the crimson worm. Jesus hung on a wooden cross. Like the worm, He gave His life to save His children. You and I are His children.

The word used for *worm* in this psalm paints an entire picture of Jesus' sacrifice. By shedding His blood, He gave us life. This is an *Easter Egg* within an *Easter Egg*. There is not one but two hidden pictures of Jesus inside Psalm 22.

Keeping the crucifixion of Jesus in mind, read Psalm 22:7–13 again.

**Now read the following verses from the gospels and write down the similarities you see to Psalm 22:7–13.**

### Matthew 20:19

### Mark 10:34

### Mark 14:65

### John 19:3

**Luke 22:63**

Now read Psalm 22:14–18. Around 1,000 years before it happened, the psalmist's description of Jesus' crucifixion continues with great detail. By this time, after hanging on the cross for several hours, Jesus would have been utterly exhausted. He would have been physically, emotionally, and psychologically poured out like water.

*All my bones are out of joint* (Psalm 22:14, ESV): Scholars tell us the shoulders, wrists, and even elbows would have been pulled out of joint from the extreme trauma of the cross.

*My heart is like wax; it is melted within my breast* (Psalm 22:14, ESV) is the quote. The distress would have caused fluids to gather in the sack around the heart and lungs. We know the Roman soldier would later puncture Jesus' chest cavity with a spear. Water and blood would flow out.

*His strength was failing*: He tries to push himself up by his feet and wrists to be able to draw a labored breath. Due to total exhaustion and inability to get their breath, most victims of crucifixion would die of suffocation.

It was a horrific way to die. And it is like David was there giving us a front row seat to the entire appalling event.

*My tongue sticks to my jaws* (Psalm 22:15, ESV): We know it as a sign of dehydration and extreme thirst.

**Read John 19:28. What does Jesus say?**

*Those mocking him surrounded him like dogs just waiting for him to die* (Psalm 22:16).

*They have pierced my hands and feet* (Psalm 22:16, ESV): David's writing accurately depicts the process of crucifixion, even though that method of killing was not used in his day.

**Read Luke 24:39. What does Jesus tell the disciples to look at to prove it is Him?**

*They divide my clothes* (Psalm 22:18, NIV®).

**Read Mark 15:24. What are the soldiers doing with Jesus' clothes?**

As a little bonus, Roman soldiers were able to divide the belongings of the crucified among them. That is what Mark records, and it is what David prophetically recorded 1,000 years before it happened.

God has included in the Old Testament, written 1,000 years before it took place, a glimpse of Jesus on the cross. There are nuggets of truth here for us: Jesus understands us, Jesus sacrificed for us, Jesus was mocked for us, and Jesus suffered for us. It is not pretty, it is hard to read, and it leaves us with a mixed bag of emotions. But the crucifixion of our Savior is something we must face. This leaves one big question: "What will you do with Jesus?"

Will you let this reminder of what Jesus did on the cross inspire you to new heights of worship and reverence? Will you see in this miraculous prophecy the final piece that breaks through to you and inspires you to claim Jesus as your Savior? Will you be reminded of all Jesus paid to make a way for your sins to be forgiven? Will this motivate you today to finally get serious about your walk with Christ and abandon the sin you have continued to entertain?

**Read Isaiah 53:5. What will you do with Jesus?**

**What step do you need to take in response to His sacrifice?**

As you end this chapter, write a prayer asking God to help you step into the new life He made possible through His sacrifice. Be sure to spend some time in thanksgiving for who He is and what He gave for us!

# Lesson 7: A Royal Psalm

## Psalm 110

In Lesson 6 we directed our gaze toward the cross. We followed the words of the psalmist across time from Old Testament to New Testament as he prophesied the sacrifice of our Messiah. Now, we get a front row view of his power.

Psalm 110 is considered a royal psalm. When a psalm is identified as a royal psalm, it has a simple goal of celebrating and exalting God as King.

**Read Psalm 110 in its entirety. Write down your thoughts as you read.**

Some scholars think this psalm once again speaks of the Messiah. In the opening verse the psalmist says, *The LORD says to my Lord*, meaning "God says to the Messiah." The psalmist viewed the coming Messiah as his Lord. In verse 1, the Lord of the psalmist occupies the seat to the right of God, a place of high honor. God is omnipotent, and sitting at His right hand implies sitting in proximity to His great power, giving the right-hand seat bearer direct access to Him!

**Read the following verses and write down what they have to say about the right hand of God.**

### Psalm 63:8

**Psalm 20:6**

**Acts 7:55–56**

**Exodus 15:6**

Psalm 110:1 is quoted in the New Testament several times. Specifically, it is quoted in Matthew 22:44, Mark 12:36, and Hebrews 1:13. This seat is obviously a seat of honor, power, authority, and protection. It is a royal seat and the seat Jesus occupies at the right hand of His Father.

Through Jesus, we have access to the omnipotent power of God. When Jesus died on the cross, the veil of the temple was torn, giving us direct access to our God. We no longer have to go through a priest, but we can now boldly approach the throne as sons and daughters of the King of Kings!

**Read Ephesians 2. Write down what this scripture has to say about our access to the Father through Jesus.**

*We often live life in a powerless mind frame, not realizing the direct line of power we are plugged into if we are children of God. We sit—soaking in despair, hiding from the enemy as if we have lost the battle. Some of us need to pull ourselves out of the cave of defeat and stand on the mountaintop of victory with Jesus, looking out over the landscape of our lives, not with dread or fear obstructing our view, but instead, with the lenses of redemption level on our noses. Jesus won the battle, and we have access to the power, making that victory possible. When we begin to see our lives in this way, we realize that even on the hard days, even when all feels lost, we stand firm knowing the ultimate victory is already ours. We simply need a new definition of victory—one not wrapped in our own temporal expectations, but in the blood of Jesus and His eternal perspective! One where we are not seated on the throne of our lives, acting as the general in charge of the battle. But, one where our mediator, Jesus, sits at the right hand of the all-powerful General of generals, King of Kings, God Almighty! The only One who ever needs to get knocked off a throne is me, myself, and I. When He is on the throne, the battle is always won! Celebrate your King and let your life flow out of the celebration of Him!*

**—Crystal**

God is mighty in power. The enemy, Satan, has no power over Him. In verse 2, the psalmist speaks of "a rod." Many scholars believe the rod refers the gospel. Think about the darkness that can be dispelled through the power of the gospel message of Jesus Christ.

**Read the following verses and write down what they have to say about the power of the gospel.**

**Romans 1:16**

### 1 Corinthians 1:18

### 1 Thessalonians 1:5

When the gospel is proclaimed through the power and authority of God Almighty, it changes lives, rescues the dying, heals the sick, opens blind eyes, sets people free, and so much more.

The power of the gospel, however, lies within the complete message of the death, burial, and resurrection of Jesus. We cannot pick and choose the pieces of the message we find most palatable. Today we often shy away from speaking of the blood of Jesus because the violence of it makes people uncomfortable, but to do so robs the gospel of sacrifice and thereby removes the need for the resurrection in the first place. If we stop with the death and leave Jesus in the tomb, we steal the life-giving power of the gospel. And if we teach the cross only, we forego the power over death and the grave that the resurrection made possible. It is a truth where one piece hinges on the other, giving it a power unmatched by anything else in all of creation. We live because Jesus was sacrificed on the cross, died, was buried, and rose from the dead three days later. Yes, we live because He lives, but we also live because He died. This is the power of the Gospel living inside of all of us. The gospel is a rod in the hands of our mediator, Jesus, who has the power to defeat even the greatest of enemies.

**How has the power of the gospel changed your life? Do you feel comfortable sharing the gospel with others? If so, write down a time when you felt the power of the gospel working in the life of someone you shared it with. If not, write down what you believe the barrier is in your life preventing you from sharing the gospel with others.**

We have all had times in our lives where we found it easier than at others to talk with someone about faith. Probably most of us could say we have walked away from a conversation at least once in our lives where we felt like we missed an opportunity to share the gospel with someone. We are called to make disciples, but the truth is, it's not always easy. Some feel more comfortable sharing than others. We all are gifted in different ways, and sometimes we use that exact logic to make excuses about why we don't share our faith. However, according to the Word, making disciples is our great commission as children of God.

**Read the following scriptures and write down what they say about sharing the gospel.**

### 1 Peter 3:15–16

### Psalm 96:2–4

**Matthew 28:18–20**

**2 Timothy 1:7–8**

God's Word does command us to share our faith, but sharing is also the fruit of a growing child of God producing in them a "willingness" to do what their Father asks of them. If you look at Psalm 110:3, it speaks of a people who offer themselves freely to the Lord, a people fully surrendered to serving their King.

**Read the following scriptures and write down what each one says about serving God.**

**Colossians 3:23–24**

**Romans 12:1**

**Romans 12:11**

**1 Samuel 12:24**

**Psalm 100:2**

Read Psalm 110:3 (ESV) one more time and notice at the end what it says about *the dew of your youth*. There is a youthful radiance and joy coming from the life of an individual serving God with a willing heart.

**Who do you know that has the radiance of a willing servant of God, and what is it about them that represents this for you?**

There is beauty in a life surrendered fully to God, the Father, just as there was certainly beauty in the life of Jesus fully surrendered to His Father. We are to be a reflection of Jesus to a lost world, giving them a glimpse of the peace found in dwelling beneath the powerful right hand of the King of Kings. The peace we find in the service of a King who always keeps His Word is indescribable, especially in light of the world we live in today.

So many rulers and individuals in authority these days say one thing and do quite another behind closed doors. This generation would say authority figures who lie, cheat, and steal are more often the rule than the exception. But we serve a Heavenly King who is who He says He is and does what He says He will do. When He makes an oath, it is sealed in eternity with the weight of all of heaven behind it.

**Read Psalm 110:4 and write down what was promised.**

To understand this oath, you have to dig a bit, which I would encourage you to do in order to learn more about Melchizedek and the symbolism within the mention of his priesthood. We will only do a shallow dig.

The priests of the psalmist's days were all descendants of Aaron. What's interesting is God gives us a picture of a priest who predates Aaron. In Genesis 14 we see a short glimpse of this man named Melchizedek who is described as Priest of God Most High.

**Read Genesis 14:17–21 and write down what you see in the interaction between Abram and Melchizedek.**

There is much debate about Melchizedek. (We will call him "Mel" for short.) We only see him in three books of the Bible; however, he is mentioned ten times in those three books. We see him first in Genesis 14, then here in Psalm 110:4. The other eight mentions of Mel are found in Hebrews 5, 6, and 7. We will not spend time here to dive into all the ins and outs of our friend, Mel. But, let me just simply say this: Melchizedek is one of a very few people in the Old Testament whose genealogy is not included.

Mel serves as a type of Christ—someone we draw correlations to through the similarities between him and Jesus. Mel does not have a predecessor or a successor according to what we know about him. And if you read Hebrews, you will see the comparison of Mel and Jesus. There was no Messiah before Jesus, and there is no Messiah after Him. He always has been and always will be the Messiah. The Alpha and Omega. Beginning and End. He just is. He is the forever reigning Lord seated at the right hand of the Father, all-powerful King of Kings. Jesus serves as the forever High Priest for His people! This is the power we have access to.

**Read 1 Peter 2:9. According to this scripture, who are we and what should we do because of who we are?**

As children of God, a chosen people, and part of the royal priesthood, we are to declare praise to our King. The rest of Psalm 110 speaks of the might of our great Redeemer. There is so much to be celebrated about our God, about Jesus! He is King, and He is worthy of our praise.

**End your time in the Word today by writing down all you discovered about your King and the access you have to His power.**

**Write down any revelations you have had about the way you live in response to being a part of the royal priesthood.**

**Now, write a prayer celebrating the might of the King of Kings!**

# Lesson 8: A Messianic Psalm

## Psalm 98

It is fitting to follow our study on Psalm 110 with a look at Psalm 98. We ended Lesson 7 with writing a celebratory prayer for our King of Kings. We begin Lesson 8 by reading Psalm 98, which is a study in celebrating our God. There is even a mention of the right hand of God in this psalm just as in Psalm 110.

**Read Psalm 98. Write down your thoughts as you read.**

What do Andy Williams, The Supremes, Bing Crosby, Ella Fitzgerald, Johnny Cash, Nat King Cole, Walter Cherry, Neil Diamond, Pat Boone, Perry Como, Mariah Carey, and the a capella group Pentatonix all have in common? They all have recorded a version of the old Christmas carol, "Joy to the World." This song was originally written by Isaac Watts in the year 1719. Although it was written over 300 years ago, today it is the most published, most popular Christian hymn in North America. What you might not know is this song was inspired by Psalm 98.

The words to Psalm 98 were relevant during the days of the psalmist. They were relevant in the year 1719 when Isaac Watts penned the words to "Joy to the World." And they are relevant for us today.

**Read Psalm 98:1 again and write down why the psalmist says we should be singing.**

**What God had done up until the time this psalm was written was most definitely worth singing about. When the psalmist originally wrote this, what was he thinking about?**

Certainly, the story of God's people in captivity in Egypt occupied his thoughts. This was a story central to God's people. It was passed from one generation to the next. God sent Moses and worked through him to perform miracle after miracle. If you know the story, you know about the ten miraculous plagues: water into blood, frogs, lice, flies, livestock deaths, boils, hail, locusts, three days of darkness, then finally the death of the firstborn children (see Exodus 7—8). These were impossible acts, done with the ultimate result of God's people being saved from bondage. God's people were set free!

The psalmist writes about what God has done, and he envisions what God would do as he writes about the day salvation would come in the form of a Baby who would become the Messiah, the Savior of the world.

**Read Psalm 98:1 again. What does it say God's right hand and arm have worked for?**

In the original language, this is the idea that God has saved His people from ruin, from destruction, from harm. He says God's right hand and His holy arm have "worked" salvation. The psalmist is painting a picture for us.

*There is a picture painted here of strength. What do you think of when you see someone with chiseled arms—where you can see every muscle? It tells you that person has power. They can probably pick up, move, and do some things you can't. There are some guys and girls at the gym that walk in, and you just know during the work out they are going to be doing some things we won't be doing. God Almighty has "chiseled" all-powerful hands and arms that worked salvation for us!* **—David**

But what difference does any of this make? The saving victory that God brings is established by His power. He did it. He arranged it. He made it happen. His right hand and His holy arm worked salvation. It's only by God's power that salvation comes. Only a powerful God could bring about our salvation through the virgin birth of His Son, Jesus! God sent His Son to save you.

Millions of people in our world don't think they need God. You might be one of those. But we do need God. We can't save ourselves from this broken, temporary world. Our bodies are frail, our time is limited on this earth, but Jesus has come, sent by God as our Savior! He has come to save you!

Humanity has accomplished some amazing things in this world. We can build skyscrapers, send people to the moon and back, land a rover on Mars, and check out the pictures it sends back.

We can build bionic arms and legs and hearts; we can print 3D body parts and map the human genome (don't know what that means, but it sounds really cool). We are working on self-driving cars, which could honestly be a life-saving advancement for some people who have no business driving a car. The greatest human invention of all time is probably a toss-up between duct tape and the seedless watermelon!

Humanity is amazing but we cannot save ourselves. No matter what other religions teach about karma and good works, living a life earning God's favor or tipping the scales with our good deeds will never be enough.

The awesome news of great joy for all people is this: Jesus was born to save you!

**Read John 3:16 and write down what God did and why He did it.**

A messianic psalm is one that prophesies of Jesus, the Messiah—the One who would save us all. Mary, the mother of Jesus, must have recognized the fulfillment of this psalm as she sang her song after being told she would give birth to the Messiah.

**Read the first part of Psalm 98. Then read Mary's song in Luke 1:46–55. Write down the parallels of these two portions of scripture.**

Mary gave birth to the Messiah. Our salvation was born and grew to be a man. Jesus then made known His salvation to His disciples as they spent time with Him, were taught by Him, and watched the miraculous things He did. He gave sight to the blind, healed lepers, fed the 5,000, and raised the dead—just to mention a few of His miracles. As the disciples walked with Him, they began to understand Jesus was not just another rabbi. He was indeed the Messiah.

**Read Matthew 16:15–16. Who did Simon Peter say Jesus was?**

As Jesus stands before them, the disciples realize He is their Messiah. They are literally looking at their salvation. But Jesus did not come just to be their salvation or ours. He came to save the world.

**Read Psalm 98:2–4 again. Who has seen the salvation of God and who is to sing with joy?**

God's plan has always been to make a way for humanity to reconnect with Him, to find a way for our sin to be dealt with. If we study human history and overlay the events recorded in the Bible, we can see a grand redemptive story. In Psalm 98:3 (ESV) we read, *He has remembered his steadfast love and faithfulness to the house of Israel.*

The Israelites wandered around in the wilderness constantly disobeying God, but He did not give up on them. In the original language, the word *steadfast* is used to show that God did not give up on His stubborn, rebellious, stiff-necked people as they wandered around in the wilderness. Steadfast love is part of the character of God. It is central to who He is.

Then the psalmist says prophetically, *All the ends of the earth have seen the salvation of our God* (Psalm 98:3, ESV). God's heart is to save the world—not just the Jews. Not just people in a certain nation. Not just people with a certain skin color or racial background. Not just religious people. Not just church people. Jesus came to save tax collectors and prostitutes. He came to save the proud and the humble, the grouchy and the happy. He came for the liberal and the conservative. The steadfast love of God is for everyone!

**Read the following scriptures and write down what they say about God's love.**

**Psalm 143:8**

**1 John 4:7–11**

**1 John 3:1**

God's love is deep and wide for the world. So vast in fact, He gave His Son to atone for all our sins. There is no greater love than this. He loves us so much that His plan for us is to spend eternity with Him. One day, He will send Jesus back to get us!

**Read Psalm 98:4–9 again.**

Verse 9 prophetically speaks of the Messiah returning to judge the earth. Again, here is the psalmist in a prophetic, forward-looking posture, writing about what will one day happen. Christ was sent by the Father to become one of us. Born in a manger, living among us, He was tempted like us yet lived a sinless life. He gave His life on a cross, died, then three days later rose again. He went back to the Father but make no mistake—He will come again!

We can ignore the truth. We can try to run from the truth, but the day is approaching. As we look around this world, we see the brokenness in it. We see the injustice, violence, racism, and on and on. It's a crazy world, and it's only getting worse. There are humanitarian crises across the globe in Syria and the South Sudan. Central American countries in turmoil like El Salvador, Honduras, and Guatemala. Nations plagued with violence and gangs. Human trafficking across the globe, right here in the United States, and probably in your own city. There are stories of people doing horrific things—crazy, mind-blowing stories that almost don't even shock us anymore.

But in Psalm 98 and in other scriptures, we are reminded that Christ, the Savior, is coming again and He will make all things right. Every sin will be paid for. We can pay for it ourselves and spend eternity separated from God, or we can accept the payment Jesus made on the cross, receive His amazing grace, and live with Him for eternity.

He has come to save you. He has come to save our world. And as He comes again, He is coming to save you from this world to spend eternity with Him.

**Read the following scriptures and write down what they have to say about eternity.**

**1 John 2:17**

**Romans 6:23**

**Galatians 6:8**

This world is not our home. This is all temporary and fleeting. But God has worked salvation for us! The Christmas carol, "Joy to the World" we referenced in the beginning of this lesson has a line in it that says, "Let every heart prepare Him room."

Have you made room for Jesus? Have you accepted the salvation worked on your behalf, for you, for our world, to save us from this world?

If not, please turn to page 105 for the plan of salvation then return to this page and write down the date and time you took the step to accept this gift. Then be sure to share your decision with someone in your life.

Date I accepted Jesus: ____________________ Time: ______________________

If you have already accepted this gift, write a prayer of praise just as Mary did when the angel told her the Messiah was coming.

Consider sharing this good news with someone who does not know Jesus. It is the greatest gift you could ever give! Write down the name(s) of someone who needs this gift of salvation, and ask the Lord to open the door for you to share with them.

# Lesson 9: A Psalm of Praise

## Psalm 33

We ended Lesson 8 looking intently at eternity and our acceptance or denial of the gift of salvation. If you have accepted the salvation worked for you by God Almighty, then you have a reason to praise Him! Psalm 33 is a praise psalm. A song sung in praise produces a sweet aroma in the throne room of our Holy God.

**Read Psalm 33 and write down your initial thoughts.**

If I were to ask you if you were thankful for God, you would more than likely say yes. Somehow this idea of being thankful and living a joy-filled life gets lost in translation. Often our thankfulness for God and all He is and has done doesn't quite make it to our faces or affect our actions.

Have you ever heard of the "frozen chosen?" I hate to say it, but this is what many believers are called. Our faces stiff, our sense of humor locked safely away so as not to seem too insincere, our ability to relate to our world and the people in it lost somewhere in the pool of judgment in which we are standing knee deep. We have frozen out the joy of life. Have we ever considered that the loss of our joy as children of God might actually be one of the reasons our world cannot see Jesus clearly? Our frosty attitudes have steamed up the windows of the warm hearts of love we were intended to share with the world.

According to Psalm 33, it is "fitting" for those of us who know the Lord to praise Him. Most of us would say we want to have a thankful heart and live a joy-filled life no matter the circumstances. And most of us would say we do a good job of being thankful on good days. The issues begin to arise when life throws us a curve ball. You see, being thankful is inextricably bound to trust. Trusting God in the hard times allows us to stay thankful because we know in the end He has us in His hands.

I am not saying you have to be thankful for the circumstances surrounding your hard times. Instead, let your thanksgiving flow from your ability to see God walking with you in them. Be thankful for Him in all circumstances. Therein lies the difference. We let the circumstances circumvent our thanksgiving. What if we started allowing our thanksgiving to God to circumvent our circumstances?

**Read the following scriptures and write down what you learn about being thankful.**

**Colossians 3:15**

**Colossians 3:17**

**Psalm 107:1**

**Philippians 4:6**

Expressing thanksgiving to God is different for everyone. Some express their thanksgiving out loud, some in silence, some through song, some through playing an instrument, some through prayer, some through writing, preaching, teaching, or serving. In Psalm 33, the psalmist mentions singing, shouting, and playing instruments. The vehicle for your thanksgiving is between you and the Lord.

The key is to find a vehicle of praise for the Lord, and be sure to drive it daily, taking a different route occasionally or the drive becomes "old hat," causing you to lose interest. Failing to drive your vehicle of thanksgiving daily can produce a rusty vehicle, and eventually the engine will die all together or be difficult to start up. You may even want to choose a new vehicle of thanksgiving in order to keep your thanksgiving drives vibrant.

**Read Psalm 33:3 again. What kind of song are we to sing to Him?**

This verse says to sing a "new" song to Him. After studying this verse in particular, I think this simply means to look for new, fresh ways to see God and be thankful. Don't continually sing the same song of praise. Be aware of His presence and activity in your life daily and look for new ways to praise Him. Work to find new ways to experience the attributes of God. If worship music is your all-time "go to" for praise, switch it up and go for a praise walk. If prayer is your normal vehicle of praise, then try playing an instrument, if you are musically inclined. If being in nature is your vehicle of praise, try serving somewhere in your church or community to express your praise and thankful heart. Your journey with God is meant to bring newness to your life. He is so vast you could never experience all there is to know of Him. Find your vehicles of praise, use them frequently, use them differently, but be sure to use them all! It's meant to be more of a motor pool than a one car garage. Enjoy the drive!

**What are your "vehicles" of praise? How do you express praise to God?**

**What is a new way you might consider praising Him?**

The psalmist now switches his thoughts from the admonition to praise to the reason why we should praise.

**Read Psalm 33:4–22 and write down the reasons why we should praise God.**

**Now read these scriptures and write down why these writers say we should praise God.**

**Isaiah 25:1**

**Psalm 139:13–14**

**Psalm 63:3–4**

**2 Corinthians 1:3–4**

**Daniel 4:37**

God's greatness is revealed in who He is, in what He does, in how He loves, in His Word, in His creation, and in many other ways.

**How is God's greatness most often revealed to you?**

**Read Psalm 33:6 again and write down how the heavens were made.**

*Psalm 33:6 is one of my favorite verses in this portion of scripture. To think, just simply by the words from His mouth, all of creation came into existence. I cannot even fathom the power in His voice. The majesty of the vision of mountains rising into the sky because God decided He wanted a mountain range in Tennessee. Try to imagine the cold, blue water filling the Great Lakes just because our Great God thought it would be the perfect place for it. He is an Artist unmatched by the greatest of all painters. He is a Creator no human inventor could ever possibly rival. The songs He placed in the mouths of the birds, on the legs and wings of insects, and in the low whistle of the breeze blowing through the trees no composer could ever hope to match. He is a great, big, almighty God whose thunderous voice can create and destroy. He shouts in thunder and whispers in the wind. Yet He loves us tenderly enough to color the petals of the most delicate rose and dust it with a fragrance soft and sweet. Oh, how I love Him. Oh, how I marvel at Him.* **—Crystal**

**Read the following verses and write down what you learn about the voice of God.**

### Psalm 29:3–9

### Ezekiel 43:2

### Hebrews 12:26

The psalmist goes on from the power of the voice of God to the oceans, nations, and the fear of the Lord, and the help He is to those who fear Him. Pointing out that mankind cannot hope to be delivered by the might of their own hand or the strength of their armies, the psalmist concludes the Lord and His unfailing love is their only hope.

We talked about the salvation provided through Jesus in Lesson 8. We talked about the power of salvation being worked for us by the strong right hand of God Almighty. Yes, this is our ultimate hope, but God is powerful in so many other ways as we have seen in scripture. He is a powerful warrior on our behalf if we fear Him.

When speaking of "the fear of the Lord," the Word of God is referring to a healthy reverence of God as God. We are to sit in awe of Him—marveling at His greatness—not because He needs us to bolster His holy self-esteem but instead because we need it. We need to remember just how amazingly awesome He is every day in order for our fickle hearts to stay true to our trust in Him. When you truly have a healthy view of the greatness of God, you can do nothing but trust Him, sitting in reverence, awe, and fear.

**Read Proverbs 14:26–27 and write down what you learn about the fear of the Lord.**

Hope and confidence come from the heart that fears the Lord. The psalmist ends by affirming his hope in the Lord.

**Read Psalm 33:20–22 and write down what the psalmist says about his hope.**

You see, there is a secret sauce to this whole recipe for praise. The secret sauce is desperation. When we truly realize how desperately we need God, how great He truly is, and then we firmly grasp that this great, Almighty God steadfastly loves us, we can do nothing but praise!

**At the end of your time today, write your own psalm of praise to the Lord.**

# Lesson 10: A Psalm of Wisdom

## Psalm 1

We have reached our last lesson in this study on Psalms and have learned many things from the writers of this rich book of poetry. In the beginning we talked about repentance. Later we talked about the salvation possible through Jesus. In Lesson 9 we talked about the greatness of God, the fear of the Lord, and the praise He deserves. We will end our time together looking at a topic that can sometimes be uncomfortable––how to live holy lives in the midst of an unholy world.

We like to be in control. We have authority issues. We most definitely do not like someone telling us what we should do or how we should live. But God is not just anyone. His Word has quite a bit to say on the subject of holiness or right living. And let me just remind you as we get started: God's advice on how to live is not about being oppressive or holding us down. It's about freedom. God's advice on how to live sets us free from and protects us from being in bondage to so many life-destroying things.

**Read Psalm 1 and write down your initial thoughts.**

The very first word in this psalm is *blessed*. In Hebrew this word is translated *esher*, which means happy or content. So verse 1 would read, *Happy is the one who does not walk in step with the wicked*, or *Content is the one who does not walk in step with the wicked*. The word *esher* is also considered to be plural, which would denote multiple blessings or a more intense level of happiness or contentment. You see, there is a higher level of contentment and happiness for those who walk in step with the Lord. There is a freedom found in the straight path that you will not find walking with the wicked.

**Read Proverbs 4:10-27. Write down what it has to say about walking with the wicked and also write down what the benefits of walking in wisdom are.**

In Psalm 1 the psalmist expands his warning just as the writer of Proverbs does in Proverbs 4. Both scriptures give pretty specific warnings. In our text, Psalm 1, he says not to walk, stand, or sit with the wicked. In other words, you should be cautious about whom you choose to pattern your life after. This does not mean you are to avoid having people in your life who are not believers. Jesus ate with people considered to be sinners, and if we are to reach the lost we cannot separate ourselves from them.

The psalmist is speaking of deeper things here: Don't follow in the footsteps of the wicked. Don't do business like them, don't live like them. Don't stand in the way of sinners. Don't do the things sinners do. Your behavior should be different. You should not mock, ridicule, or scorn others. Do not lie or live in a way that contradicts the Word of God. This scripture is about the way you live your life, the behaviors you exhibit, and the people you choose to pattern your life after.

**Read Psalm 1:2 again. Write down what the blessed one delights in and meditates on.**

The law of the Lord simply means the Word of God.

**Read the following scriptures and write down what they have to say about the Word of God.**

### Hebrews 4:12

### Luke 11:28

### James 1:21–23

### 2 Timothy 3:15–17

Something amazing happens in the life of a person who has a hunger for the Word of God.

**Read Psalm 1:3–4. Compare and contrast what the life of the blessed one looks like versus the wicked man. Write down what you learn.**

After reading Psalm 1:3, it would be easy to think that God will give His children success in all they do. This is not what this scripture means. The simple meaning behind this verse is this: In the good and bad, we can always be assured that God is with us, and we will eventually see the blessing in every circumstance if we keep our eyes focused on Him. He gives good gifts to His children, but the gifts He gives look very different from the earthly definition of gift-giving. Perspective is everything.

The last verse in Psalm 1 wraps up this psalm of wisdom in a concise summary.

**Read Psalm 1:6 again. Write down the conclusion you draw from this summary verse.**

God goes before His children. He is walking with us, and in the end He has eternity with Him prepared for us. The big difference for the wicked is the destruction they reap both here in this life and in the next.

Here's the takeaway: It matters how you live both for this life and the next. There is freedom found in a life concerned with pleasing God. When we choose to walk with the Lord, there is a contentment surpassing any satisfaction this world has to offer.

Giving your heart to Jesus is a first step, but it doesn't end there. Opening your heart further to the Holy Spirit to convict and change you from the inside out is the ongoing process of sanctification. Sanctification is a big "churchy" word simply meaning "the journey of looking more and more like Jesus." I would suggest this journey is one every believer is on until God takes him or her home to be with Him. No matter how long you have been a believer, no one has arrived at perfection on this side of eternity. We all still have room to grow.

Sometimes I think those of us who have been Christians for a long time get into a place where we believe we know all there is to know. We mistakenly think we are the perfect specimen on holy living and close our hearts to the convicting winds of the Holy Spirit to breathe new life in us. Remember, there is always room for growth!

The deeper the roots, the more fruit you can bear when God decides the time is right for you to bear it. It would be a shame for you to miss a season of bearing fruit because you decided your shallow roots were enough to sustain you. Or, for your shallow root system to fail you, knocking you off your feet, when the storms of life hit hard.

Do the daily work of growing. Do the daily work of meditating on the Word of God. Do the daily work of allowing the Holy Spirit to challenge and change you!

**As you end your time in Lesson 10, write down anything in your life you need to allow the Holy Spirit to remove or change so you can look more like Jesus.**

**Write a prayer asking God to help you do the hard work of growing deeper roots.**

# Conclusion

**You have had space in each lesson to write down some conclusions of your own. Before you put this book away, go back and look over all the lessons, come back to this page, and write down what the overall resounding message in this study was for you.**

**Now write a concluding prayer, asking God to give you what you need to live this out from this day forward.**

## Plan of Salvation

We are celebrating with you as you step into a relationship with Jesus. We want you to know you are not alone. You are not too far gone for God to pick you up, dust you off, and heal your wounds. Nobody is perfect. We are all unfinished and in process. We all mess up, and we all fall short. As a matter of fact, the Bible says in Romans 3:23 (ESV), *All have sinned*. The word *all* is important because it puts mankind in a place of humility, or at least it should. We all have a sin problem, and we all need a Savior because as it says in Romans 6:23 (ESV), *The wages of sin is death*. However, we do not need to live in this hopeless state. There is an answer.

It is important to know you do not need to have everything perfectly in order to commit your life to Christ. He wants to help you put things in order. But first things must come first. Jesus is the first thing! Romans 5:8 (ESV) says, *While we were still sinners, Christ died for us*. When we were *still sinners*, He died for you and me! The blood He shed on the cross was the sacrifice for our sin, and it has a miraculous cleansing power we have access to. This sacrifice was made possible through the love of God the Father for His children. You were so loved God gave His Son as a sacrifice (see John 3:16). The pressure is off of us to figure it all out and try to clean it all up. It's His gift to us. But we have to accept the gift; it is not forced on us.

In Romans 10:9–10, it says we only need to believe in Jesus as our Savior and confess Him Lord of our lives. There is a shift in our hearts where we take ourselves off the throne of our lives and seat Jesus there. It is a beautiful gift of freedom and life you are receiving from the God of the Universe who loves you beyond measure. And, it says in Luke 15:7 that all of heaven rejoices when you give your heart to Jesus! So today there is a heavenly party going on just for you!

Let's do this together. Pray this prayer:

Dear God, I need You. I admit I have sinned, and I am lost without You. Please forgive me of my sins. I believe that Jesus is Your Son and He died on the cross so my sins could be forgiven. I now confess Him as Lord of my life. I step down from the throne of my heart and wholeheartedly place Jesus on the throne of my life. I now ask Him into my heart and celebrate my new life in You! I accept Him as my Savior. Thank You for this gift. Thank You for hearing and answering my prayer. Help me to live my life for You from this day forward. In Jesus name I pray, Amen.

Date:________________ Time:______________ Signature:________________________________

We would encourage you to tell your pastor, family member, or friend. Find someone to walk in community with you as you grow in your relationship with Jesus. And talk with someone about baptism, which is a great next step of publicly confessing your faith in Jesus!

Again, we are so excited for you. You are loved!